THE ULTIMATE GIRLS' GUIDE TO

drawing

PUPPIES, POLAR BEARS, and other adorable ANIMALS

written by Abby Colich

illustrated by Colin Howard, Jason Juta, Juan Calle, and Stefano Azzalin

capstone
young readers

Table of Contents

Wild Animals

Perfect Pets

Fascinating Animals

Getting Started

From polar bears in the Arctic to the new puppy in your backyard, the world is full of fascinating animals. Animals are fun to learn about and fun to draw too. Whether you're skilled at sketching or new to the world of drawing, you can have fun filling pages with a wide variety of animals.

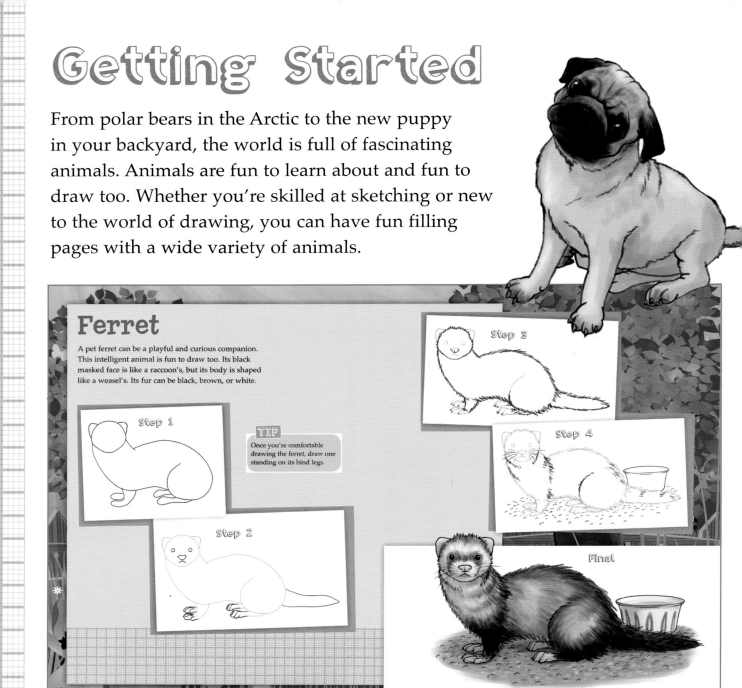

Ferret

A pet ferret can be a playful and curious companion. This intelligent animal is fun to draw too. Its black masked face is like a raccoon's, but its body is shaped like a weasel's. Its fur can be black, brown, or white.

Step 1

TIP
Once you're comfortable drawing the ferret, draw one standing on its hind legs.

Step 2

Step 3

Step 4

Final

124

125

Each activity includes a description of the animal, steps to show you exactly how to draw each creature, and a tip for when you want to get creative and mix things up. If your gorilla turns out looking like a glob or your flamingo is a fail, don't worry. Drawing takes practice. If you mess up, it's OK to start over again. Just remember to be creative and have fun while you work.

Tools of the Trade

Drawing is a fun and inexpensive way to express yourself and your creativity. Before you get started, be sure you have the proper tools.

Paper

Any white paper will work, but a sketchbook meant just for drawing is best.

Pencils

Any pencil will do, but many artists prefer graphite pencils made especially for drawing.

Color

A good set of colored pencils will give you many options for color. You can also try using markers or paint. Many artists enjoy outlining and filling in their work with artist pens.

Sharpener

Your pencils will be getting a lot of use, so be sure you have a sturdy sharpener. A good sharpener will give your pencil a nice, sharp point.

Eraser

Be sure to get a good eraser. Choose an eraser that won't leave smudges on your clean, white paper.

Electronics

Many great apps and programs allow you to draw on screen rather than on paper. If you want to give this medium a try, have an adult help you get started. Learn all the features and functions before you begin.

Sea Star

This faceless, brainless creature may seem simple, but the sea star is anything but. This animal has two stomachs—one that digests food and one that releases from its mouth to capture prey. Hundreds of tiny tube feet along a sea star's arms help it move through the water.

Step 1

Step 2

TIP

Have you ever seen a sea star with its arms bent, clinging to a rock? Tube feet help with this too. Try capturing this action on paper.

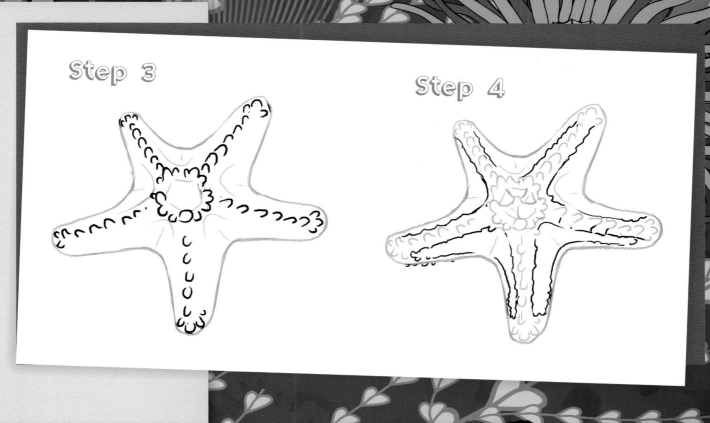

Step 3

Step 4

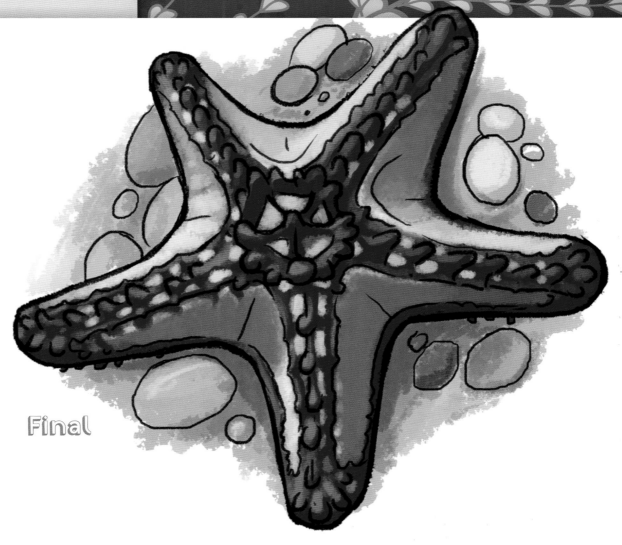

Final

Sea Anemone

Sea anemones spend most of their time attached to rocks or coral reefs. The growths coming out of their bodies are stinging tentacles. An anemone will wait for prey to come by, sting the prey with its tentacles, and then guide the meal into its mouth.

Step 1

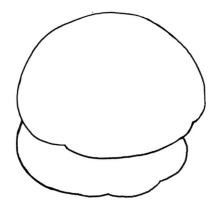

Step 2

TIP

Give your sea anemone some height by drawing it a taller body. Some anemones can be up to 6 feet (1.8 meters) tall.

Step 3

Step 4

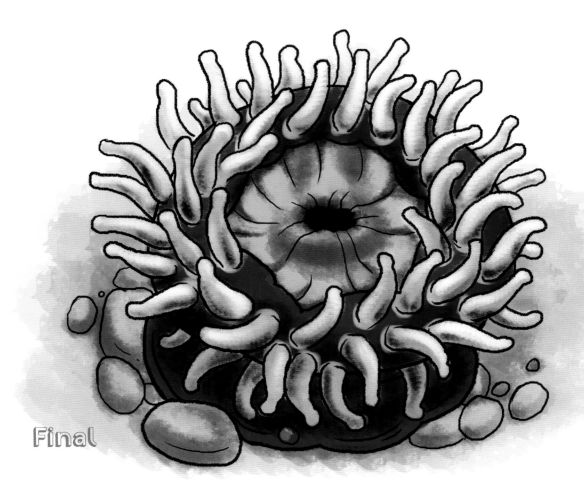

Final

Clown Fish

Beautiful, bright-orange clown fish are adorned with white stripes along their heads, bodies, and tails. Each stripe is outlined in black. A clown fish's bright skin warns predators to stay away.

step 1

step 2

TIP

Clown fish live among sea anemones. A coat of mucus protects the fish's bodies from the anemones' stings. Try drawing these two sea creatures together.

Step 3

Step 4

Final

Orca

Orcas, commonly called killer whales, are actually a species of dolphin. The largest of all dolphins, these huge creatures can grow to nearly the size of a school bus. All orcas have black bodies with white markings. Each orca can be identified by its own pattern.

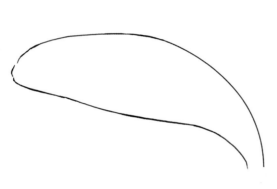

TIP

Orcas travel in groups called pods. After you learn to draw one orca, try drawing several of them together.

Step 3

Step 4

Final

Octopus

Scientists consider the octopus to be the smartest of all invertebrates. Among its many defenses from predators, an octopus can change colors to blend in with its surroundings. It also squeezes into tiny spaces and squirts out clouds of ink to hide behind.

Step 1

Step 2

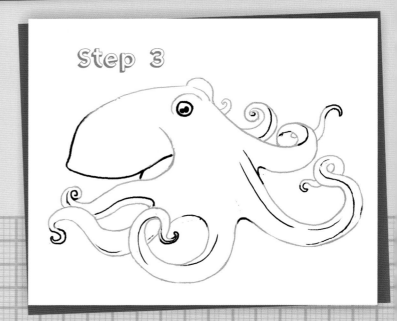
Step 3

TIP

Once you master the octopus, draw it performing one of its amazing defenses.

Step 4

Step 5

Final

Narwhal

People rarely see narwhals in the wild, but that doesn't mean you can't become a master narwhal artist. You can see why this creature is called "the unicorn of the sea." Its long horn is actually a tooth. The tooth grows into a tusk straight through a male narwhal's upper lip.

Step 1

Step 2

TIP

Be sure to draw your narwhal in an icy habitat. Narwhals only live in or near the Arctic Ocean.

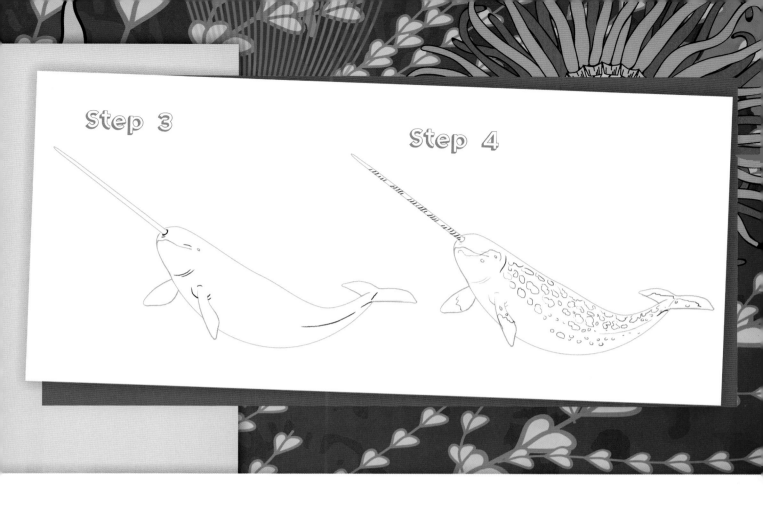

Step 3

Step 4

Final

Jellyfish

The umbrella-shaped bell, or hood, helps the jellyfish move through the water. The dark orange tentacles sting and insert tiny barbs into prey. The orange and white feathery appendages, called oral arms, begin digestion and move prey into the jellyfish's mouth.

Step 1

Step 2

TIP

A jellyfish moves through the water by expanding its bell into an almost flat shape and then closing it. Try capturing this movement on paper.

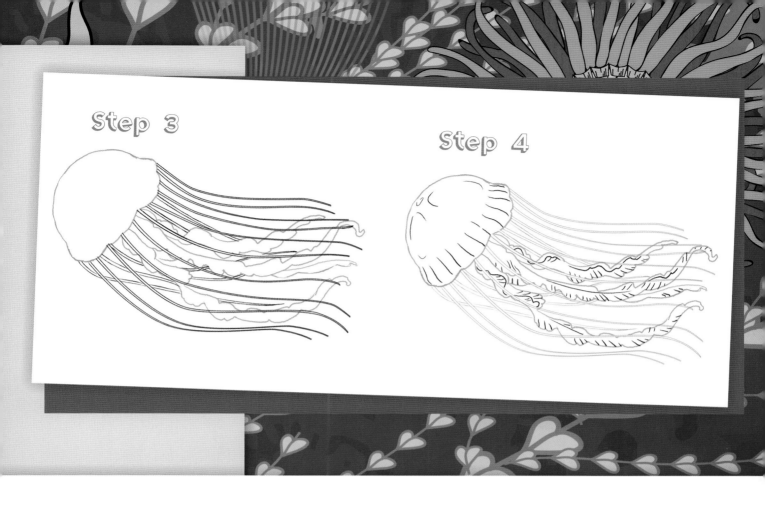

Step 3

Step 4

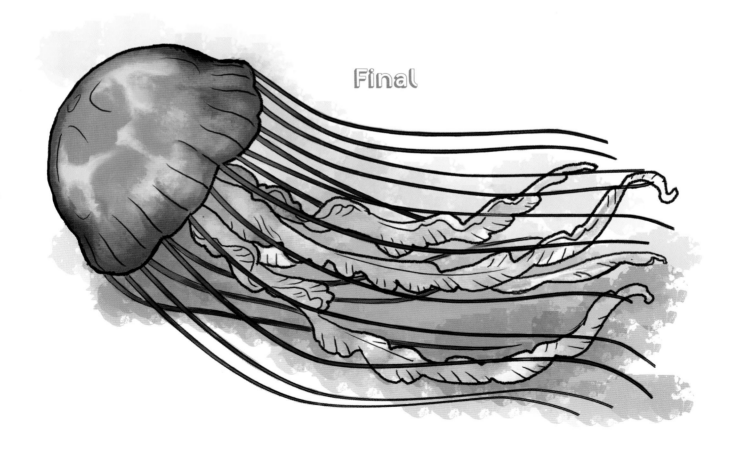

Final

Sea Horse

You can easily see how the sea horse got its name. This animal uses the little fin on its back to swim, but it doesn't go very fast. So it spends most of its time using its monkey-shaped tail to hang on to sea grass and coral.

step 1

step 2

TIP

A sea horse must eat almost constantly to stay alive. Try drawing your sea horse munching on a shrimp.

Step 3

Step 4

Final

Sea Urchin

Sea urchins look a bit like pincushions. The spines sticking out of their bodies help them move along the seafloor. The spines are also filled with venom, which helps protect the creatures from predators. Despite this defense, they can still become food for fish and sea otters.

step 1

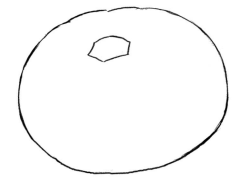

step 2

TIP

Sea urchins are actually a relative of sea stars. Draw some of these creatures hanging out together on the ocean floor.

Step 3

Step 4

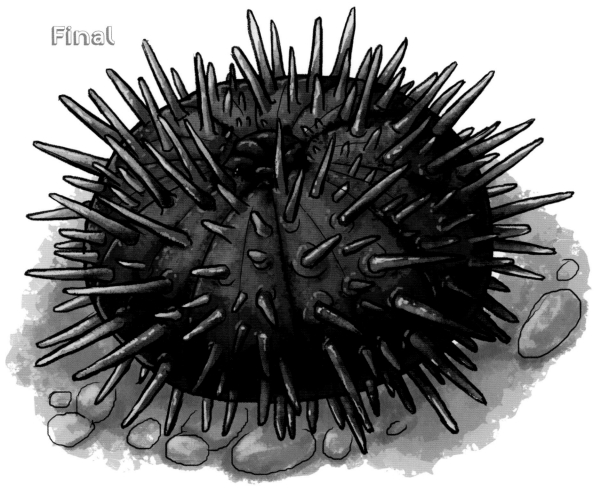

Final

Bottlenose Dolphin Family

Why do so many people love dolphins? One reason is that their curved mouths make them look like they are always smiling. You usually won't spot a dolphin alone. They live in groups of 10 to 30 called pods.

Step 1

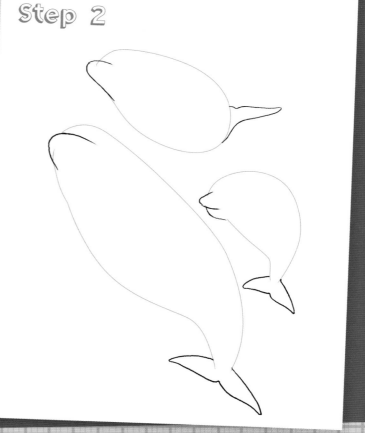

Step 2

Step 3

Step 4

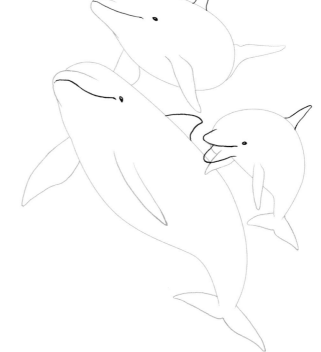

continued on next page

TIP

Dolphins must come up to the surface of the water often to breathe. Try drawing a dolphin jumping out of the water.

Step 5

Step 6

Beluga Whale

The beluga whale, or white whale, is lighter in color than its sea mammal relatives. Other differences include a broader forehead and lack of a dorsal fin on its back. Belugas are very playful and social animals, often chasing or flipping their fins at other members in their pod.

step 1

step 2

TIP

Scientists believe the beluga whale uses facial expressions to communicate. Can you draw your beluga making a different face?

Step 3

Step 4

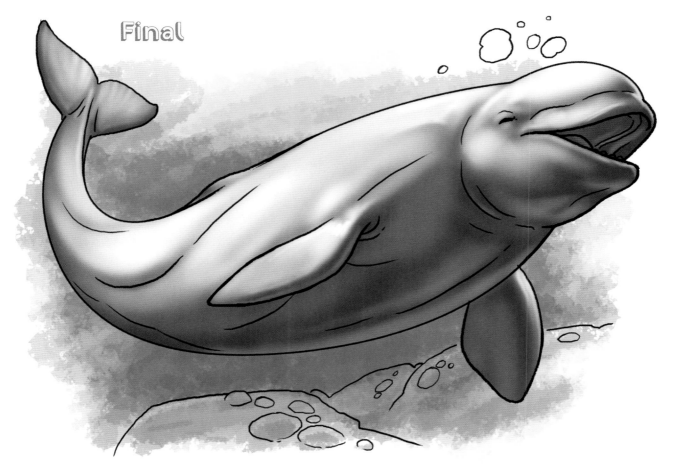

Final

Sea Otter

These mammals are well-adapted to life in the sea. Sea otters' fur repels water to keep them dry. Their webbed feet help them swim. And their nostrils and ears close up while swimming to keep water out. These smart water animals use rocks to break open clams or mussels for dinner.

Step 1

Step 2

TIP

Sea otters sometimes wrap themselves up in seaweed or kelp to keep from floating away. Try capturing this act on paper.

Step 3

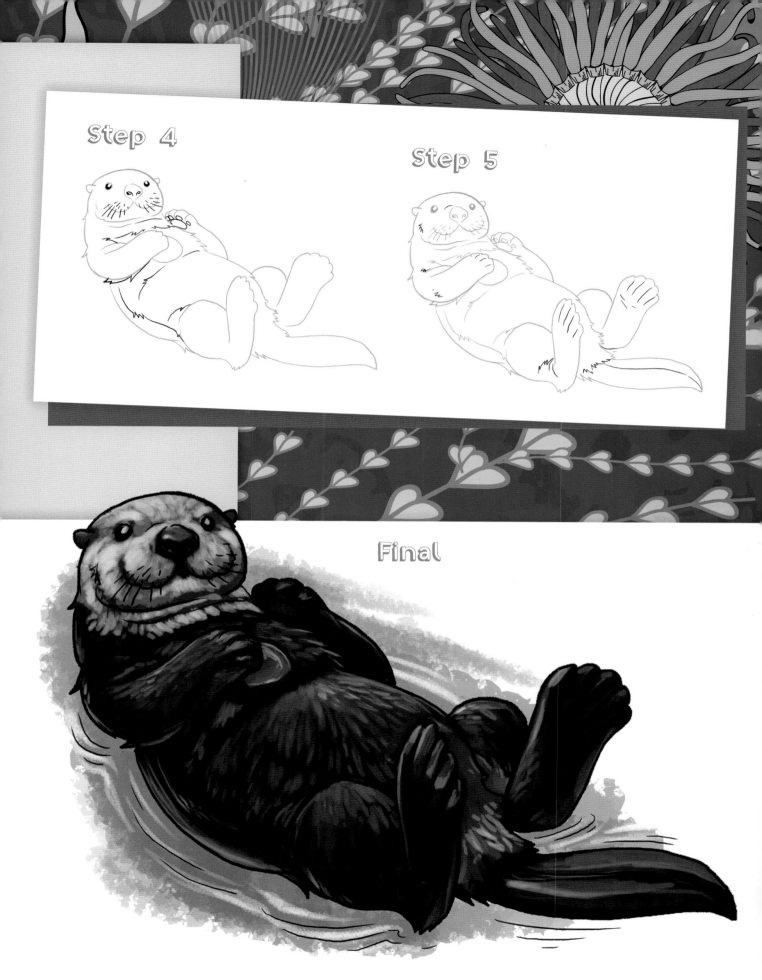

Step 4

Step 5

Final

Nautilus

This member of the mollusk family spends life inside its beautiful shell. A nautilus uses its tentacles to latch onto prey. It propels itself through the sea by sucking water into a tube on the front of its body and spitting it back out.

step 1

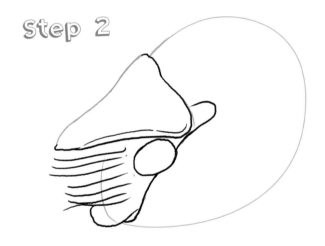

step 2

TIP

A nautilus' shell helps it hide from predators by blending into its environment. Try drawing a nautilus blending in under the sea.

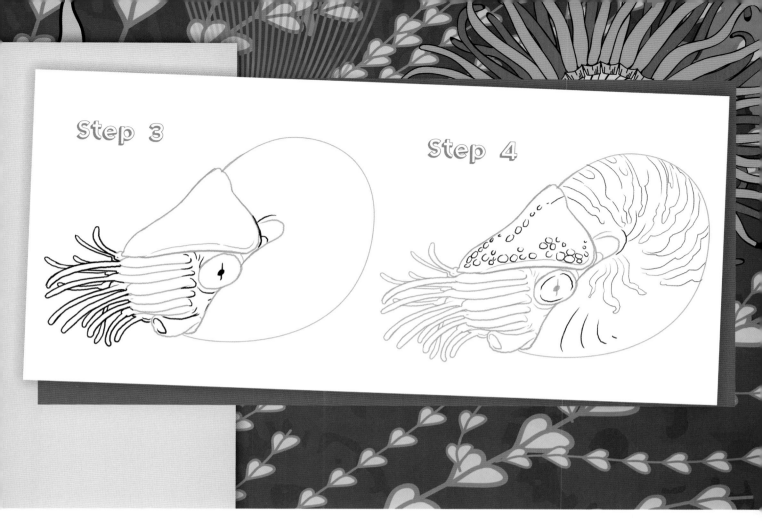

Step 3

Step 4

Final

Manatee

These gentle giants of the sea love swimming in warm, shallow water and eating plants. Their strong tails make them superb swimmers. Manatees have wrinkly faces and whiskers on their snouts. Despite their look, many people believe that sailors long ago confused manatees for mermaids!

Step 1

Step 2

TIP

Manatees have three or four little nails at the ends of their flippers. Add this detail to your drawing.

Step 3

Step 4

Final

Coral Reef

Millions of tiny animals called polyps form vast coral reefs in tropical waters. As polyps grow, they leave behind a hard skeleton. Together the skeletons create large, rocklike structures. Coral reefs are home to a wide array of creatures that form a diverse ecosystem.

Step 1

Step 2

Step 3

Step 4

continued on next page

TIP

Many creatures live on or near coral reefs, including shrimp, sea turtles, and jellyfish. Try adding one or two of these to your illustration.

Step 5

Step 6

Zebra

Known for its black and white stripes, this relative of the horse sticks out from other animals in the African savanna. Scientists believe zebras' stripes help them blend together in the eyes of their predators, making them more difficult to catch. Each zebra has its own unique stripe pattern.

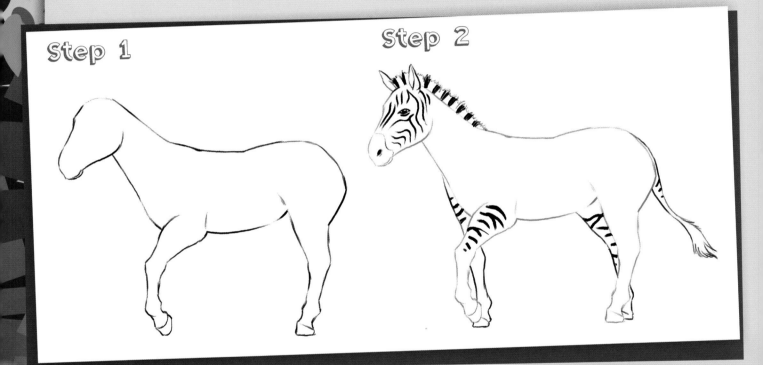

Step 1

Step 2

TIP

A zebra's stripes extend onto its short-haired mane. Don't forget this detail when drawing your zebra.

Step 3

Step 4

Final

41

Ostrich

The largest of all birds, the ostrich can't fly. But what it lacks in flying it makes up for with super speedy running. It uses its two strong legs to run from predators. An ostrich will even kick a predator with its two-clawed toes if cornered.

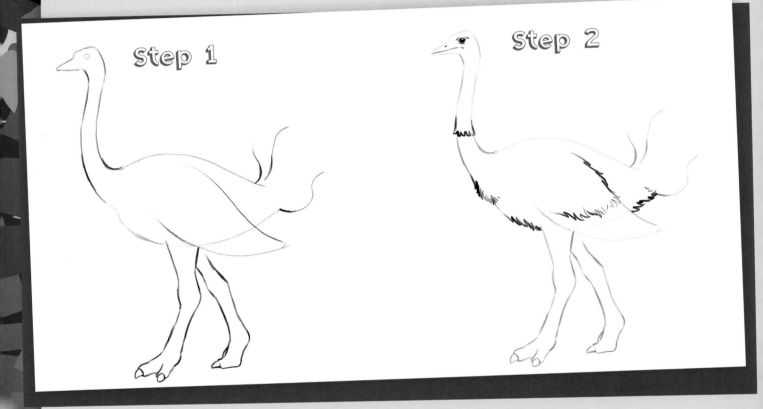

TIP

This dark brown ostrich with white wings is a male. If you want to draw a female ostrich, make all the feathers a light shade of brown.

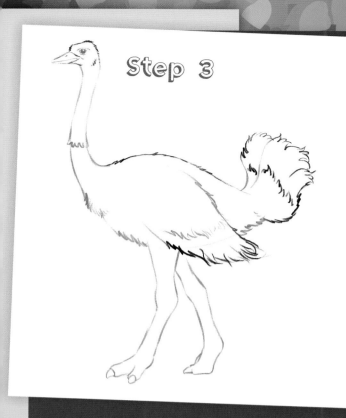

Step 3

Step 4

Final

Green Iguana

Green iguanas love eating plants and climbing trees. These lizards are covered with soft, leathery scales. Spines cover their backs from head to tail. Don't skimp when drawing this creature's tail. It can be just as long as the rest of its body.

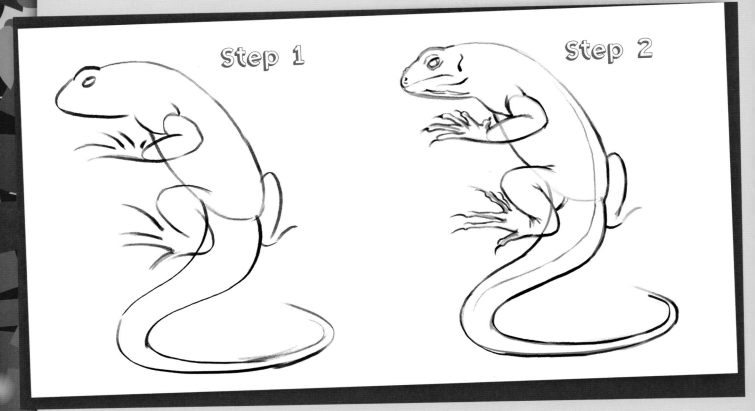

Step 1

Step 2

TIP

An iguana's strong tail makes it an excellent swimmer. Try drawing a green iguana in the water.

Step 3

Step 4

Final

45

Gazelle

The gazelle, a type of antelope, is mostly beige with a lighter underside. Some gazelles have white on their faces or darker markings on their bodies as well. In addition to being speedy runners, gazelles leap high in the air to avoid predators.

TIP

Some female gazelles don't have horns. You can draw your gazelle without them.

Step 3

Step 4

Final

Black Jaguar

Jaguars are rare in the wild, and black jaguars are even rarer. These jaguars are shiny and black all over. The biggest cat in the Americas, jaguars prowl the jungle floor hunting for food. Unlike other big cat species, they are also skilled swimmers.

step 1

step 2

TIP

Jaguars usually live alone unless they are raising young. Try drawing a mother jaguar with a cub.

Step 3

Step 4

Final

Young Elephant

Adult elephants are the largest land animals on Earth. But young elephants have some growing to do. They don't have their white tusks yet, but they do already have large ears that help them stay cool in the heat.

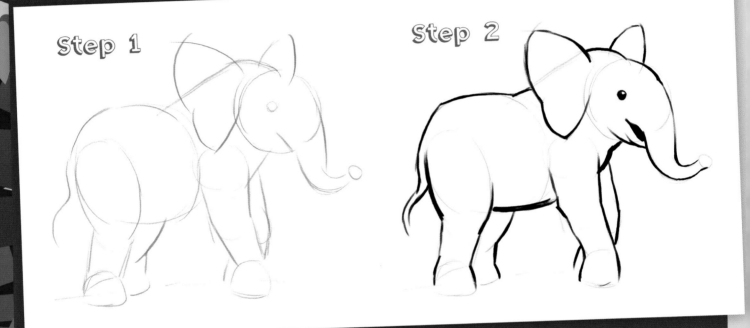

step 1

step 2

TIP

Once you've mastered this young elephant, draw one that's all grown up. Just make it larger and add the tusks.

Step 3

Step 4

Final

Gorilla

This great ape is the largest of all primates. It meanders through the rain forest walking on all fours, a movement called knuckle walking. Most gorillas are black or brownish gray. Their humanlike eyes are brown surrounded by a black ring.

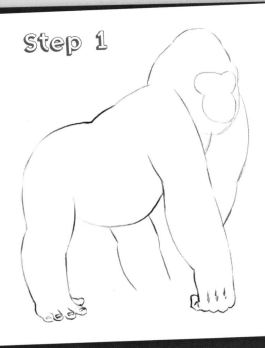

step 1

step 2

TIP

One gorilla subspecies is called the silverback. You can make your gorilla a silverback by giving its back a silver tint.

Step 3

Step 4

Final

Alligator

An alligator's body is armored in bony plates called scutes. A strong tail makes this reptile a pro at swimming in swamps and wetlands. Don't forget the nostrils on top of its long snout. These holes allow the alligator to breathe as it swims just under the surface of the water.

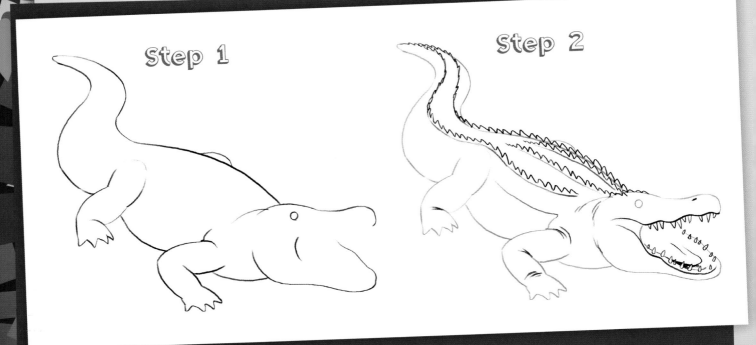

TIP

Frightened by this large creature? A younger alligator might be more your speed. Draw a smaller alligator with yellow stripes down its body.

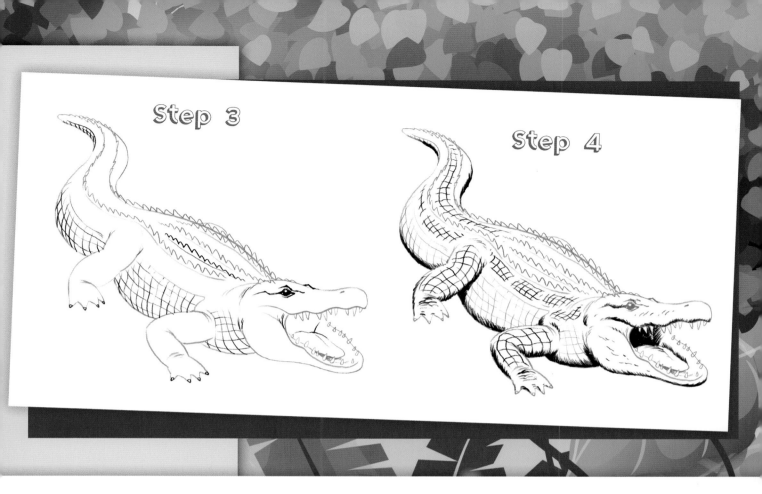

Step 3

Step 4

Final

Giraffe

The tallest animal that lives on land, a giraffe's long
neck makes it easy to recognize. This mammal's hair
is a light cream or white. Its spots are orange or brown.
Both males and females have a pair of hair-covered horns
called ossicones.

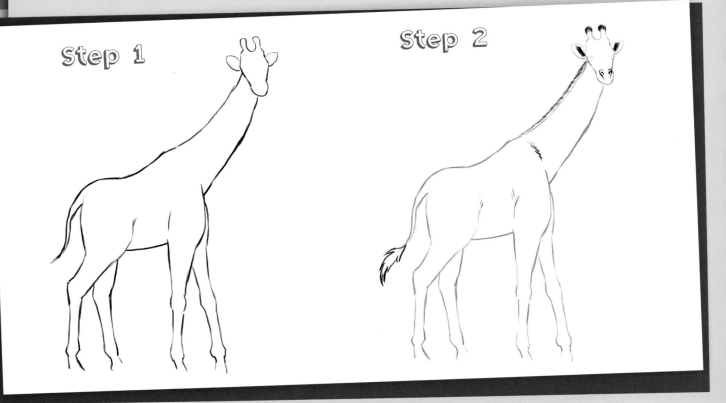

Step 1

Step 2

TIP

Each giraffe's spots are unique
like a human's fingerprints.
Draw your giraffe a companion
with different markings.

Step 3

Step 4

Final

57

Lion with Cubs

Lions are the only social species of cat, living in groups called prides. They are also the only cat species in which the males look distinctly different from the females. Brown manes encircle the heads and necks of the males.

TIP

Want to draw your cubs with their mom instead of their dad? Just draw the lion's body without the mane.

Step 2

Step 3

continued on next page

Step 4

Step 5

Step 6

Final

Polar Bear

These hunters of the Arctic have fur all over their bodies to help them keep warm. Fur is even on the bottoms of their feet to protect their paws while walking on the cold ice. Their whitish fur helps to camouflage them in the snow.

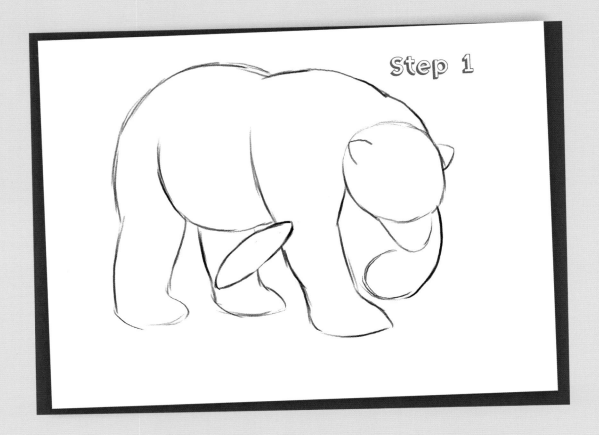

Step 1

TIP

Female polar bears usually give birth to one or two cubs at a time. Try drawing a mom with her babies in a snowy den.

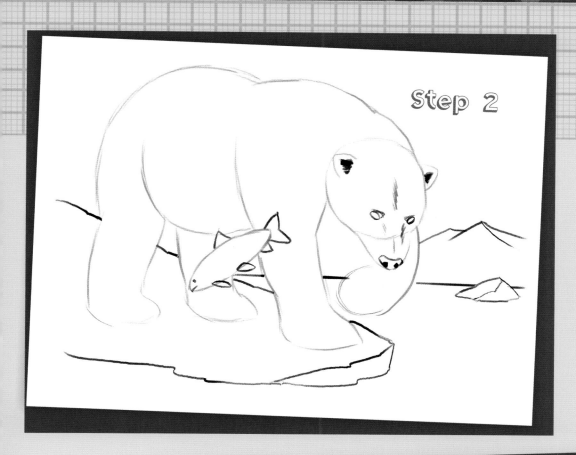

Step 2

Step 3

continued on next page

Step 4

Step 5

Step 6

Final

Orangutan

This great ape with reddish orange hair is closely related to humans. An orangutan's long arm span helps it swing from tree to tree, where it spends most of its life. It eats fruit during the day and sleeps at night in a nest made of leaves.

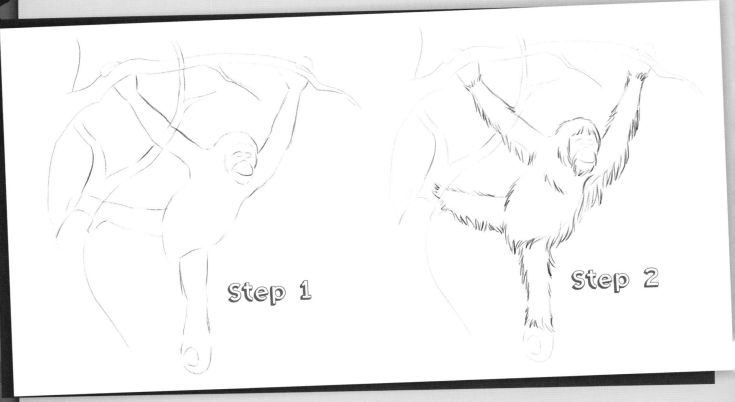

step 1

step 2

TIP

When an orangutan is standing on land, its long arms can reach the ground like a gorilla. Try drawing an orangutan in this position.

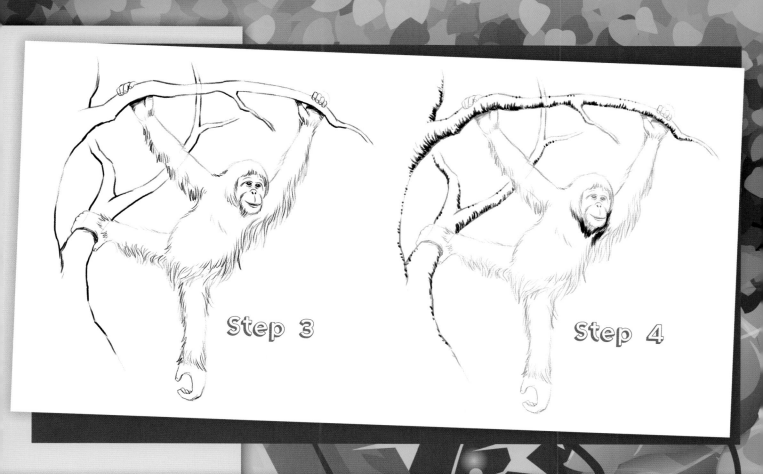

Step 3

Step 4

Final

67

Sloth

This two-toed animal has long claws that help it stay gripped to a tree branch. The sloth will live nearly all its life on a tree branch. This animal sleeps 15 to 20 hours a day. Even when it's awake, it hardly moves.

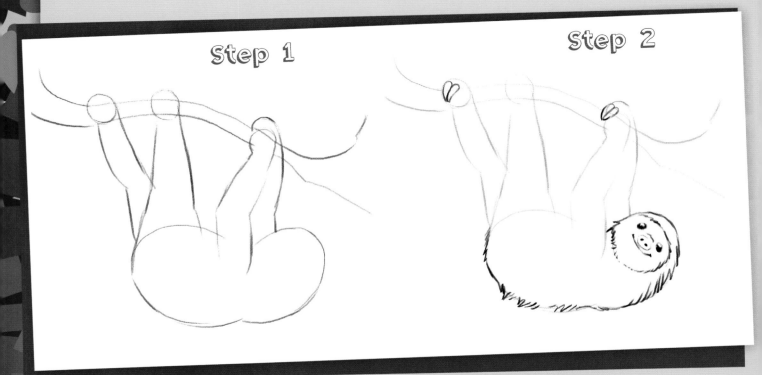

Step 1

Step 2

TIP

A sloth moves so little that algae grow on its fur. Try drawing a close-up of the sloth so you can see the tiny green growths on its body.

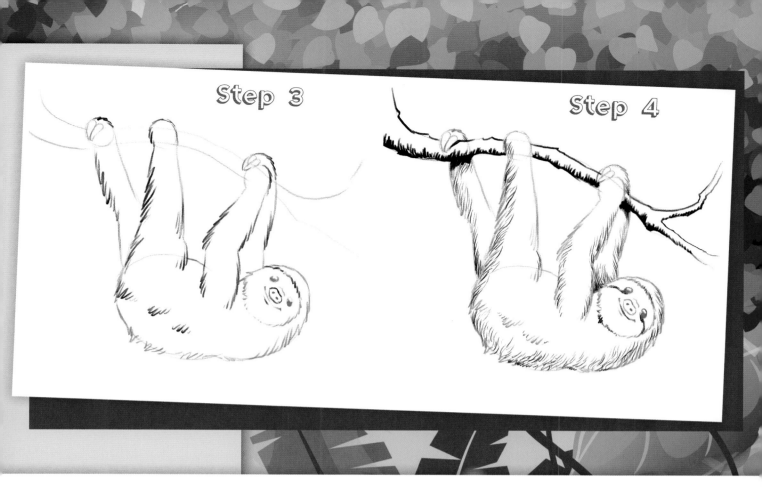

Step 3

Step 4

Final

69

Platypus

The platypus may be the world's strangest animal. It has a bill and webbed feet like a duck. It has the body and fur of an otter and the tail of a beaver. What may be most fascinating is that males can attack predators with their venomous hind feet.

Step 1

Step 2

TIP

When on land, a platypus' webbed feet pull back to reveal claws. This feature helps the platypus walk. Try drawing your platypus walking around.

Step 3

Step 4

Final

Hippo

Hippos love being in the water. Their nostrils and eyes are located on the tops of their heads, allowing them to see and breathe while spending the day submerged. Despite their short, stubby legs, hippos are the third largest land mammal.

Step 1

Step 2

TIP

Hippos spend most of the day in water or mud in order to stay cool. Try illustrating a hippo partially underwater.

Step 3

Step 4

Final

Blue Morpho Butterfly

This beautiful insect shows off four bright blue wings edged with black. Scales on the wings reflect light, giving them their blue hue. This butterfly is one of the world's largest with a wingspan of 5 to 8 inches (13 to 20 centimeters).

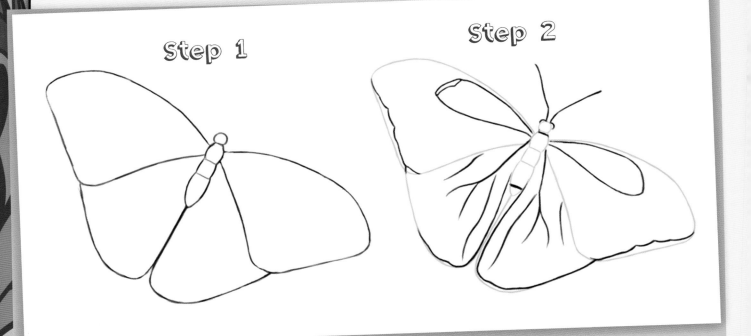

Step 1

Step 2

TIP

Draw the morpho with its wings closed. The backs of its wings are a dull brown with eyespots that help camouflage it from predators.

Step 3　　　　Step 4

Final

Blue Dasher Dragonfly

These beautiful insects are not your typical creepy crawlies. Dragonflies have four large transparent wings and slender bodies. The male dashers are blue. The females are usually black and yellow.

Step 1

Step 2

TIP

Not a fan of the blue dasher? There are plenty of other dragonfly species. Maybe the red-veined darter is more to your liking. Can you guess what color it is?

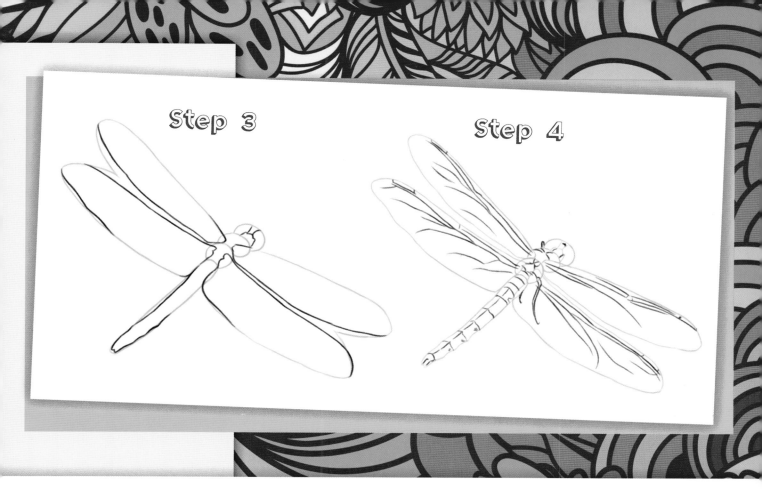

Step 3

Step 4

Final

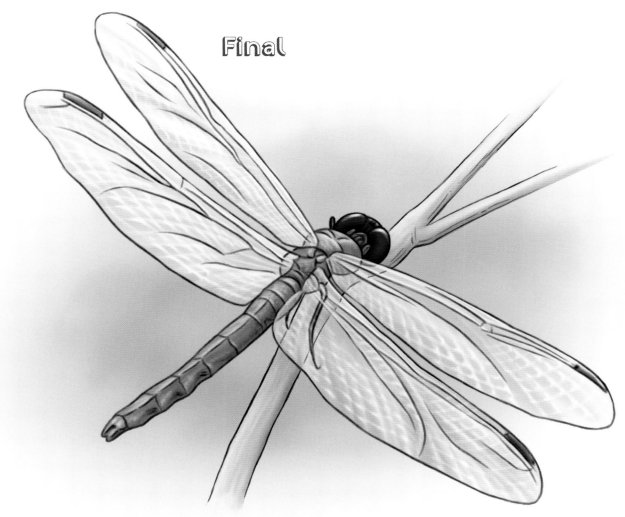

Ruby-Throated Hummingbird

These hummingbirds sport metallic green and white feathers. But only the males have a bright red throat. Hummingbirds flap their wings so quickly that they make a humming noise. Their short and stubby legs prevent them from walking or standing, so they are always on the move.

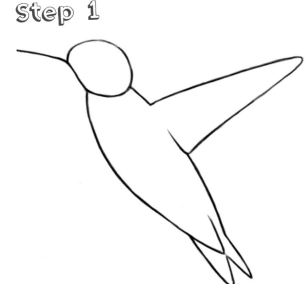

Step 1

Step 2

TIP

Hummingbirds are quite the acrobats. Can you draw one flying upside down?

Step 3

Step 4

Final

Snowy Owl

Snowy owls are born with spots that lighten as they age. Males eventually turn mostly white, while females keep some spots on their wings. Their white feathers help them blend in with their Arctic surroundings. Don't forget the sharp talons when sketching this bird. The owl uses these claws to catch prey.

step 1

step 2

TIP

Each wing of the snowy owl is longer than the length of its body. Draw this majestic bird flying with its wings spread.

Step 3

Step 4

Final

Huacaya Alpaca

Huacaya alpacas are one of two alpaca breeds. Alpacas are fluffy creatures that resemble llamas. They are raised in South America for their hair. The soft hair is used to make blankets and clothing. Alpacas come in many different shades of white, brown, and black.

Step 1

Step 2

TIP

The Suri is the other breed of alpaca. You can draw a Suri by giving your alpaca longer, shaggier hair.

Step 3

Step 4

Final

Flamingo

This pink bird spends its days wading in warm waters, usually standing on one leg with the other tucked beneath its body. It sticks its long, curved neck down into the water and grabs crustaceans with its black-tipped bill. The flamingo's diet of crustaceans turns its feathers pink.

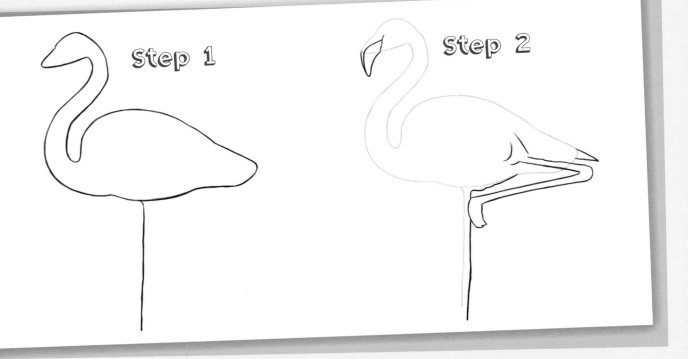

TIP

You can draw this bird in flight with its wings extended outward and its body stretched long. The undersides of its wings are black.

Step 3

Step 4

Final

Gentoo Penguin

A white-feathered cap is one of the identifying features of the Gentoo penguin. This creature also sports a bright orange-red beak and peach-colored feet. These penguins are the fastest swimmers of all diving birds, moving up to 22 miles (35 kilometers) an hour.

Step 1

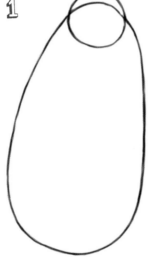

Step 2

TIP

A Gentoo penguin makes as many as 450 dives a day for food. Can you draw this bird diving into icy waters in search of a meal?

Step 3

Step 4

Final

Frilled Lizard

This lizard has an unusual feature—a flap of leathery, scaly skin around its head. When feeling threatened, the lizard opens its frill and hisses while standing on its hind legs. Then it runs on its hind legs until it finds a tree, climbing to safety.

Step 1

Step 2

TIP

Draw the frilled lizard running on its hind legs.

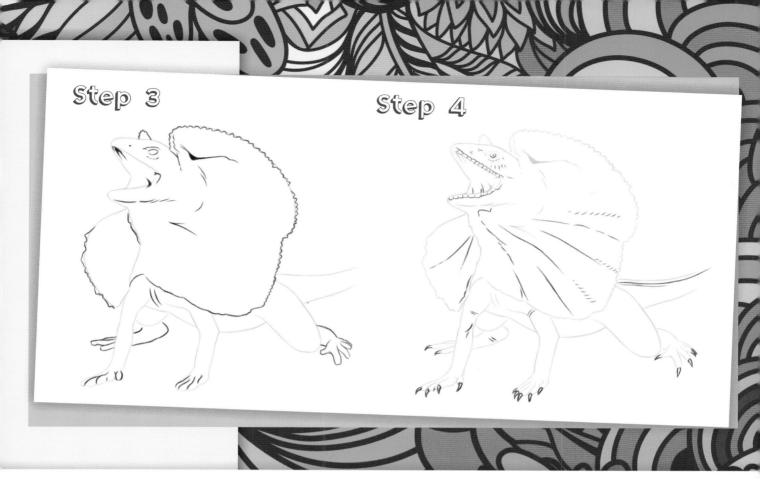

Step 3

Step 4

Final

Peacock

The peacock is known for its dramatic tail feather display. These bright feathers are covered in shades of green, blue, and gold. A dark blue marking on each feather in the shape of an eye is surrounded by other vibrant shades.

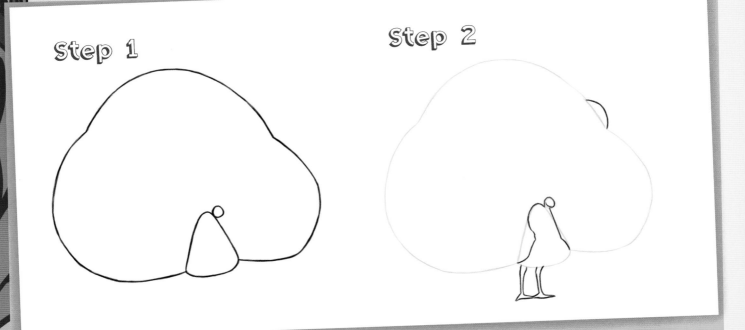

Step 1

Step 2

TIP

The peacock doesn't always walk around with its feathers upright. Draw the peacock with its feathers down behind its back.

Step 3

Step 4

Final

Capuchin Monkey

This small, furry monkey is cream or tan around the face, neck, and shoulders. The rest of its body is dark brown. It has a white or pink face and a long tail that can wrap around tree branches. Long arms and humanlike hands help this creature move around its treetop home.

Step 1

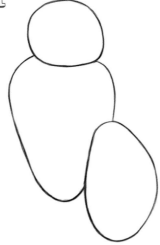

Step 2

TIP

Capuchin monkeys dig for ants with sticks and use rocks to break open nuts. Draw a capuchin using one of these tools.

Step 3

Step 4

Step 5

continued on next page

Step 6

Step 7

Snow Leopard

This rare cat has a body well equipped for life in the mountains of Asia. The snow leopard is covered in a thick white, gray, or yellow coat. Its fur is adorned with black markings called rosettes. Even its feet are covered with fur to protect its paws from the cold. Its muscular legs and tail provide the strength and balance needed to help it climb steep mountain slopes.

Step 1

Step 2

TIP

The snow leopard is a master jumper, covering six times its body length in one leap. Draw a snow leopard leaping through the air.

Step 3

Step 4

continued on next page

Step 5

Step 6

Step 7

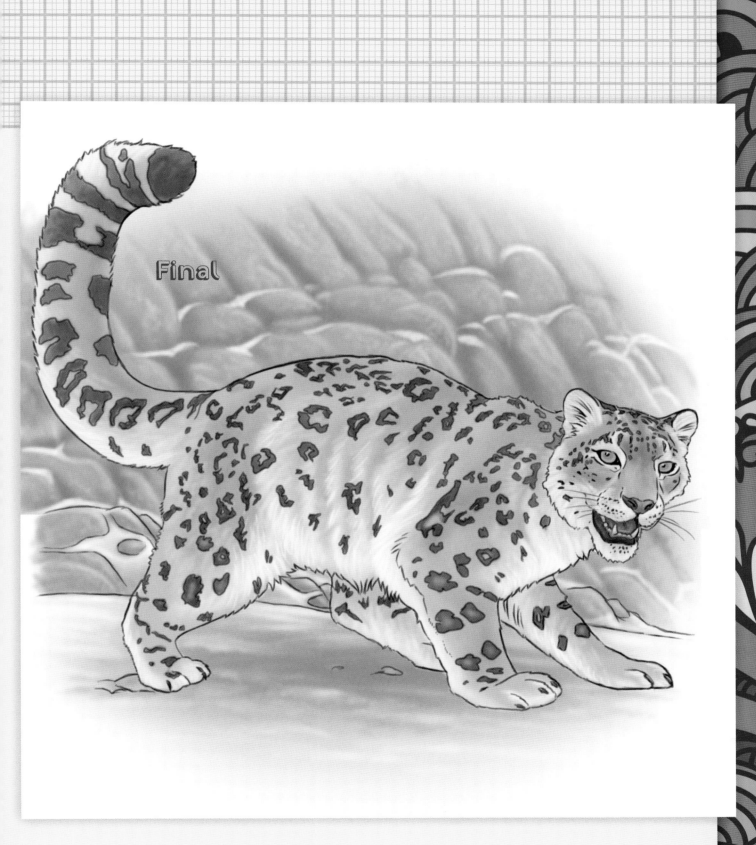

Final

Giant Panda

This black and white bear lives in the mountainous forests of China. The giant panda spends its days using its strong jaws to chew through bamboo. Pandas like to live alone and are rarely spotted by humans in the wild.

Step 1

Step 2

TIP

Pandas are usually shown sitting and munching on bamboo. But they are also excellent climbers and swimmers. Draw your panda doing one of these activities.

Step 3

Step 4

Final

Spotted Deer

The spotted deer has a brown or reddish coat, a white underside, and white spots. Spotted deer have short tails, and males have two long antlers. Also called chitals, these animals graze in the forests and grasslands of India.

Step 1

Step 2

TIP

A spotted deer will stand on its hind legs to reach the leaves of a tree. Try capturing this on paper.

Step 3

Step 4

Final

Koala

Koalas are fuzzy, tree-climbing marsupials. Females carry their young in a pouch, much like kangaroos. Koalas have claws with an opposable digit, much like a human thumb. This feature helps them climb eucalyptus trees where they look for leaves to eat.

Step 1

Step 2

Can you draw your koala curled up for a nap? Koalas spend up to 18 hours a day sleeping!

Step 3

Step 4

Final

Mute Swan

The graceful mute swan swims along the water with its long neck outstretched. Covered in white feathers, this bird is truly beautiful. Its bill is orange with black stripes and a little bump at the top. The mute swan got its name because it is so much quieter than other swan species.

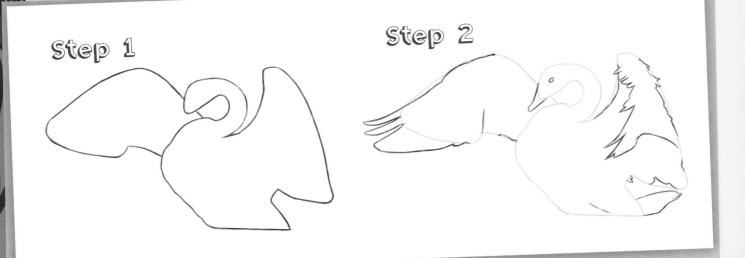

Step 1

Step 2

TIP

Another popular species is the black swan. Color your swan black with a bright orange or red bill.

Step 3

Step 4

Final

Betta Fish

Betta fish, also known as Siamese fighting fish, might be aggressive to other fish, but they are lovely to watch. These fish come in many gorgeous colors, including oranges, reds, blues, and greens. You can capture their vibrant shades best when you draw their large, flowing fins extended outward.

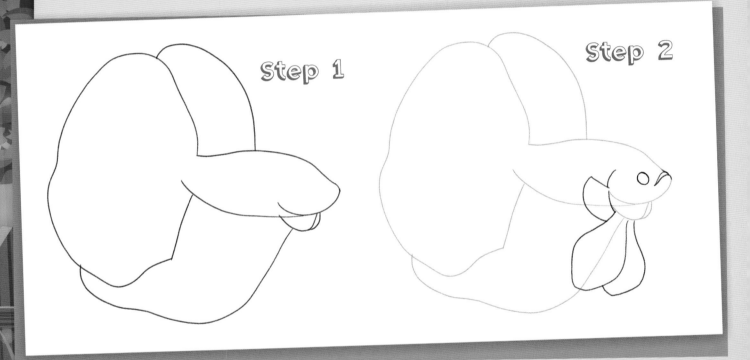

Step 1

Step 2

TIP

Try drawing a betta with its fins down at its sides. It is just as colorful and beautiful!

Step 3

Step 4

Final

Hamster

The cute and fluffy hamster is so small it can fit in the palm of your hand. This rodent comes in a variety of sizes and colors. Its paws look like tiny hands. Don't forget this detail when drawing this fun pet.

Hamsters need exercise! Draw a wheel with your hamster running inside it.

Step 3

Step 4

Final

Hermit Crab

Think a hermit crab is a boring pet that stays in its shell all day? Think again! Even though a hermit crab likes the inside of its shell, it comes out at night to eat and play. You might even get to see your crab move to a bigger shell or molt its skin.

Step 1

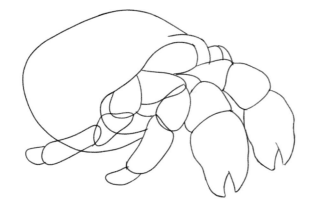

Step 2

TIP

Despite their name, hermit crabs like to be social. Draw one or two friends for your crab.

Step 3

Step 4

Final

Tree Frog

If you own a tree frog, then you know to keep it wet. But you can stay dry while drawing this amazing amphibian. Have fun as you fill in the neon green body, blue markings, red eyes, and orange feet.

Step 1

Step 2

TIP

Tree frogs love to climb! Draw your frog climbing up a tree.

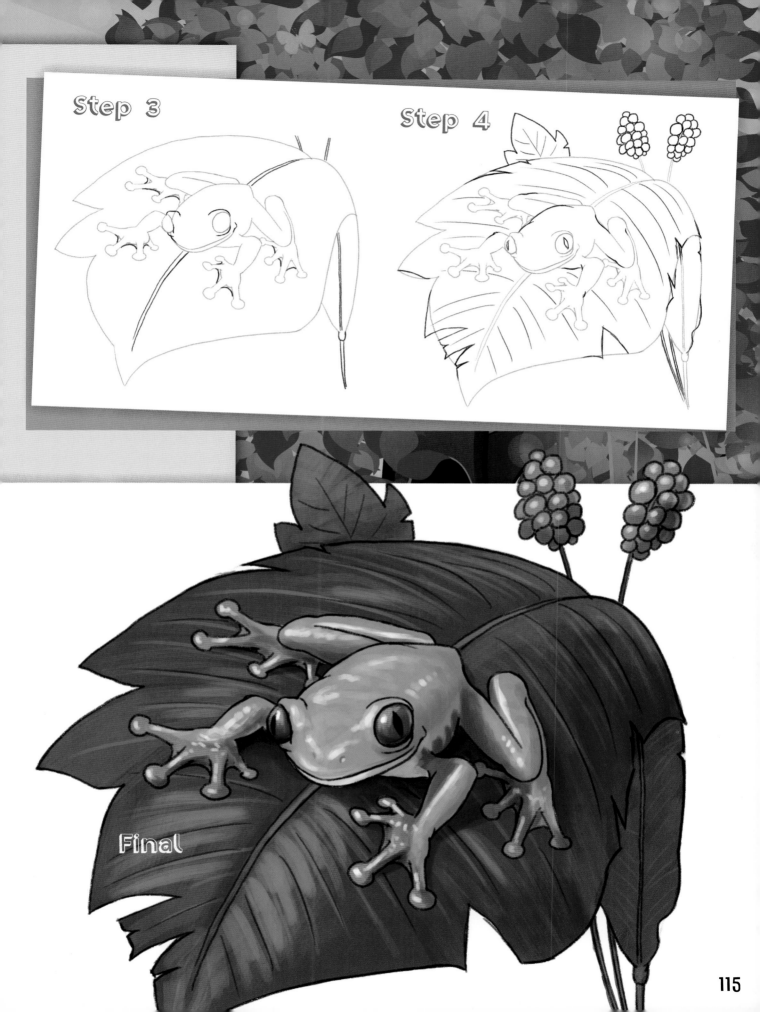

Step 3

Step 4

Final

Parrot

The parrot is the only pet you can teach your language! Whether perched in its cage or on your shoulder, it may want to chat as you sketch. Be sure to draw the beak curved and pointed. This feature helps the parrot crack open hard nuts.

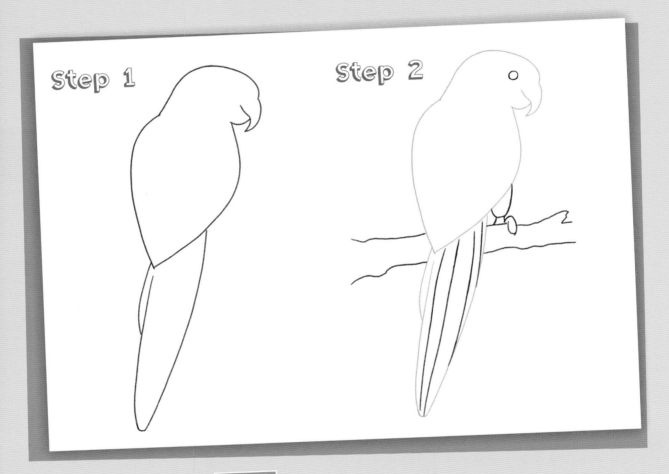

Step 1

Step 2

TIP

Parrots come in many bright colors. Experiment with different shades.

Step 3

Step 4

Final

Rabbit

A pet rabbit is cute and cuddly. Even though your paper and pencil aren't soft and furry, you can still have fun drawing this pet! Its floppy ears and cottonlike tail may be your favorite features, but don't forget the whiskers!

Step 1

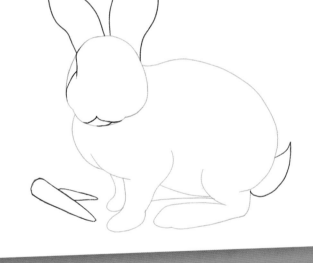

Step 2

TIP

Pet rabbits like to hide under furniture. Can you draw a rabbit peeking out from under your bed?

Step 3

Step 4

Final

Pug with Puppies

What's cuter than a pug? Pug puppies, of course! Sketch these dogs with their wrinkly faces, boxy bodies, and curly tails. Most pugs sport a shade of light brown fur called fawn, but they can also be black, gray, or white.

Step 1

Step 2

TIP

Draw one of your pug puppies playing fetch with a tennis ball.

Step 3

Step 4

continued on next page

Step 5

Step 6

Final

Ferret

A pet ferret can be a playful and curious companion. This intelligent animal is fun to draw too. Its black masked face is like a raccoon's, but its body is shaped like a weasel's. Its fur can be black, brown, or white.

Step 1

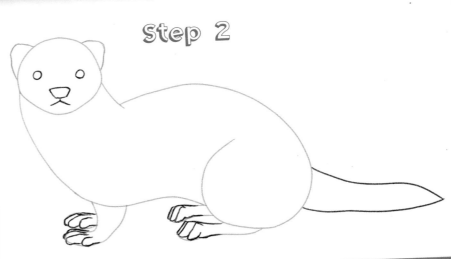
Step 2

TIP

Once you're comfortable drawing the ferret, draw one standing on its hind legs.

Step 3

Step 4

Final

125

Cat

Cats are playful and mischievous creatures. They'll scurry across the floor chasing their toys, hide in a corner, and jump from high spaces. Then they'll curl up next to you for a nap. Capture the amazing life of a pet cat in this sketch.

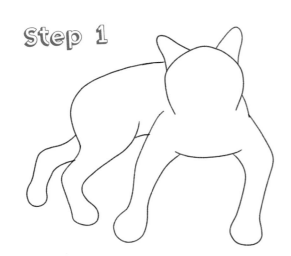

step 1

step 2

TIP

Cats always land on their feet when jumping from high spaces. Try drawing your cat making a smooth landing.

Step 3

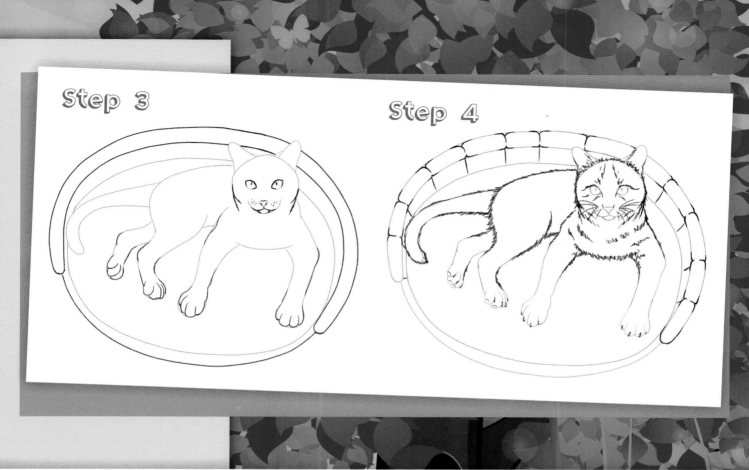

Step 4

Final

Horse

Shiny, beautiful hair growing from a long, flowing mane is just one majestic quality of the horse. Their personalities show through in their facial expressions. When you re-create this beautiful being on paper, be sure to catch it in its graceful gallop.

Step 1

Step 2

TIP

Once you master the horse, add a saddle and reins.

Step 3

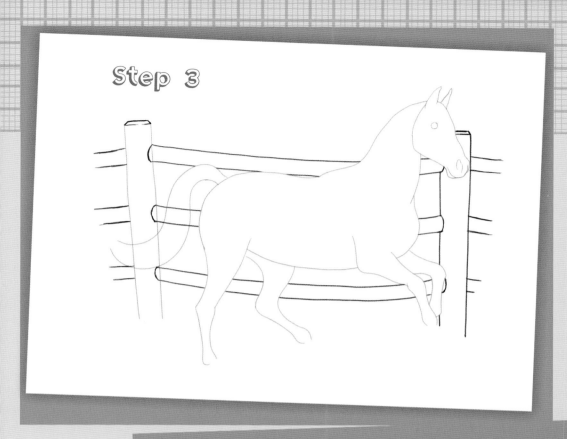

Step 4

continued on next page

Step 5

Step 6

Final

Leopard Gecko

Geckos climbing up the sides of their tanks are fun to watch. The tiny suction cups on their feet give them this ability. Be sure to give your gecko's skin a rough and bumpy look. These bumps, called tubercles, help protect the gecko in its natural habitat.

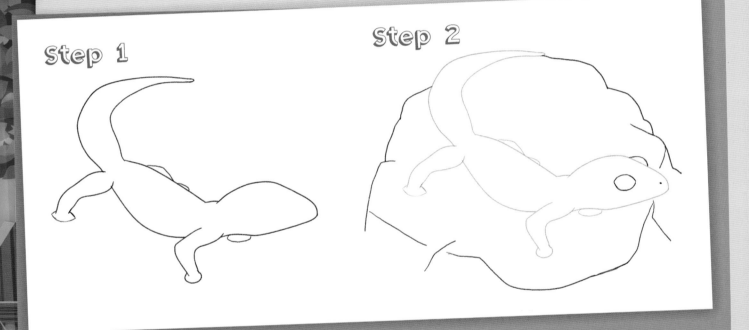

Step 1

Step 2

TIP

Give your gecko a different pattern or play around with different color variations.

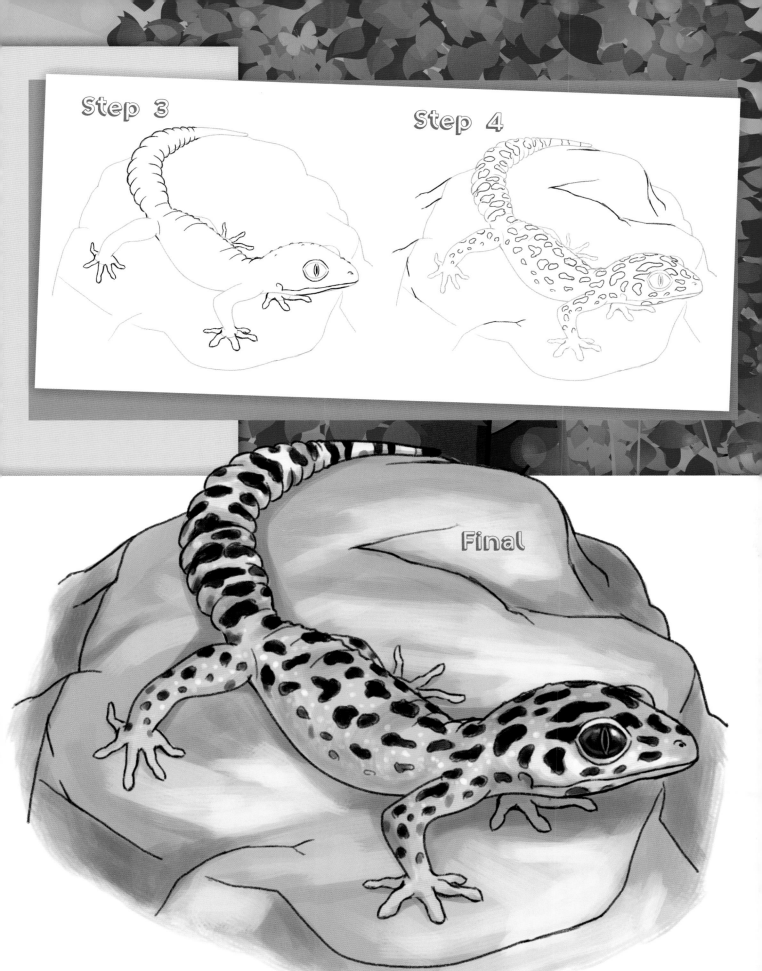

Step 3

Step 4

Final

Turtle

Whether flopping through the water or basking in the warm light, turtles make interesting pets. The scutes, or plates, on a turtle's back are shaped like hexagons. Not only do scutes help protect a turtle, but they also tell scientists how old it is.

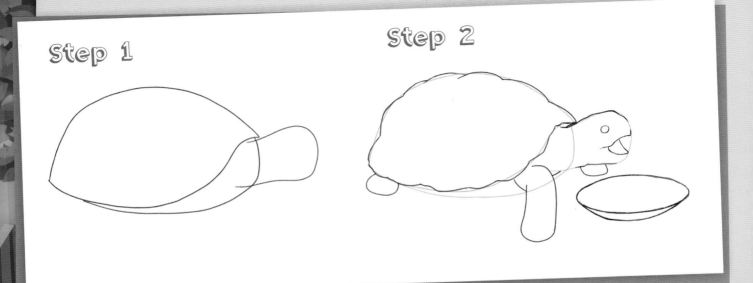

Step 1

Step 2

TIP

Don't get scared and hide in your shell! Get adventurous and draw your turtle swimming around outside in the water.

Step 3

Step 4

Final

Gerbil

Gerbils are social animals that love to interact, especially with their human owners. Gerbils might look like mice, but they have smaller ears and furrier tails. The most common pet gerbil, the Mongolian, comes in 20 different shades and patterns.

Step 1

Step 2

TIP

Gerbils need to burrow. Can you draw one burrowing in its bedding?

Step 3

Step 4

Final

Corn Snake

Slithery and scaly, the corn snake is the most common snake kept as a pet. Corn snakes usually come in patterns of orange and black, but they can be many other colors as well. These calm and easygoing snakes like sliding around their tanks looking for places to hide.

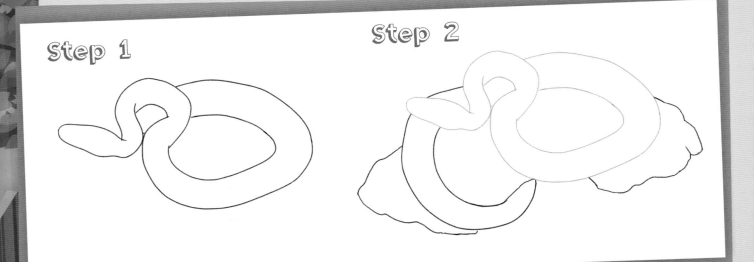

Step 1

Step 2

TIP

This pet snake loves being held by its owner. Draw yourself holding your pet snake.

Step 3

Step 4

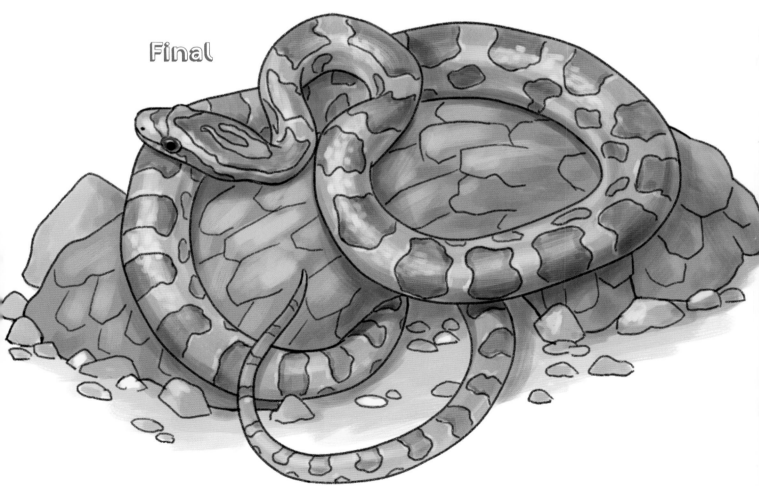

Final

Tropical Fish Tank

Colorful fish swimming to and fro. Plants swaying back and forth. A sea star resting on a rock. Put this beautiful scene together by drawing a tropical fish tank. Take your time sketching the details, and have fun filling in the colors.

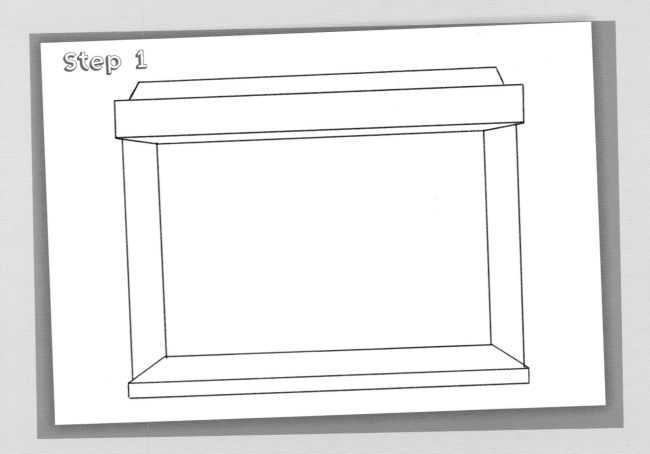

Step 1

TIP

Do you know how to draw any other fish tank creatures? Perhaps a shrimp or a little eel? Try adding these to your tank.

Step 2

Step 3

continued on next page

Step 4

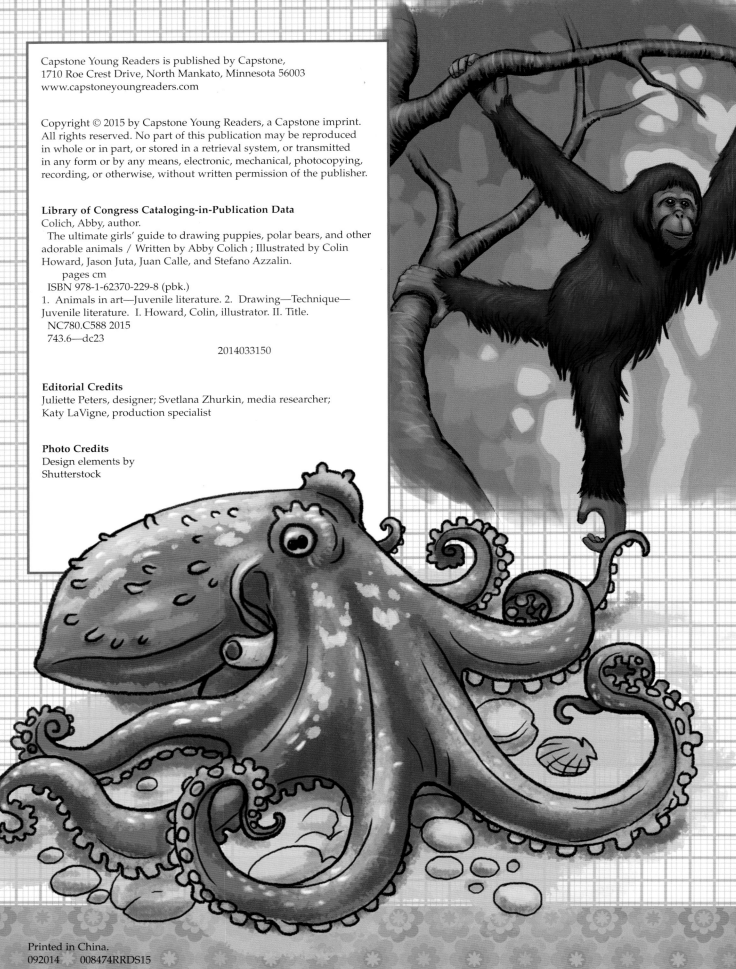

Capstone Young Readers is published by Capstone,
1710 Roe Crest Drive, North Mankato, Minnesota 56003
www.capstoneyoungreaders.com

Library of Congress Cataloging-in-Publication Data
Colich, Abby, author.
 The ultimate girls' guide to drawing puppies, polar bears, and other
adorable animals / Written by Abby Colich ; Illustrated by Colin
Howard, Jason Juta, Juan Calle, and Stefano Azzalin.
     pages cm
  ISBN 978-1-62370-229-8 (pbk.)
 1. Animals in art—Juvenile literature. 2. Drawing—Technique—
Juvenile literature. I. Howard, Colin, illustrator. II. Title.
  NC780.C588 2015
  743.6—dc23
                          2014033150

Editorial Credits
Juliette Peters, designer; Svetlana Zhurkin, media researcher;
Katy LaVigne, production specialist

Photo Credits
Design elements by
Shutterstock

Printed in China.
092014   008474RRDS15

GET YOUR PENCILS AND PAPER READY!

You'll love drawing these animals from all over the world. Step-by-step illustrations will guide you through drawing animals from the Arctic to your own backyard. Every project will help you CREATE SOMETHING UNIQUE.

$14.95 US $16.95 CAN

ISBN 978-1-62370-229-8

51495

9 781623 702298

capstone
young readers
capstoneyoungreaders.com